ANIMAL PLANET

BIG ANIMALS
STICKER FUN

Miles Kelly

First published in 2005 by Miles Kelly Publishing Ltd
Harding's Barn, Bardfield End Green, Thaxted, Essex, CM6 3PX, UK

This edition printed in 2012

2 4 6 8 10 9 7 5 3 1

Publishing Director Belinda Gallagher
Creative Director Jo Cowan
Project Manager Lisa Clayden
Edition Editor Amanda Askew
Cover Designer Kayleigh Allen
Designer Tom Slemmings
Reprographics Stephan Davis
Production Manager Elizabeth Collins

British Library Cataloguing-in-Publication Data
A catalogue record for this book is available from the British Library

ISBN 978-1-84810-845-5

Printed in China

COVER Keith Levit/Shutterstock, tl Eric Isselée/Shutterstock,
BACK COVER cl Eric Isselée/Shutterstock; 2bl Four Oaks/Shutterstock;
2br Eric Isselée/Shutterstock
All other images are from the MKP archives

www.mileskelly.net
info@mileskelly.net

www.factsforprojects.com

INTRODUCTION

Big animals live all around the world, from the freezing Arctic to the sandy deserts of Africa. Lots of big animals are endangered. People are afraid that some will become extinct (die out completely) and are trying to save them.

There are big animals such as whales and sharks living in the ocean. Huge birds such as the wandering albatross soar in the skies, while on land there are enormous elephants.

With this great sticker book you can learn all about big animals and amaze your friends with fun animal facts!

Mini stickers!

Which animal is the world's largest predator? What do golden eagles like to eat? How long can a walrus tusk grow? Use your mini stickers to find out about big animals underwater, on land and in the air.

In the water – many huge animals live underwater
In the air – these birds can fly high in the air
On the land – some animals spend most of their time on the ground

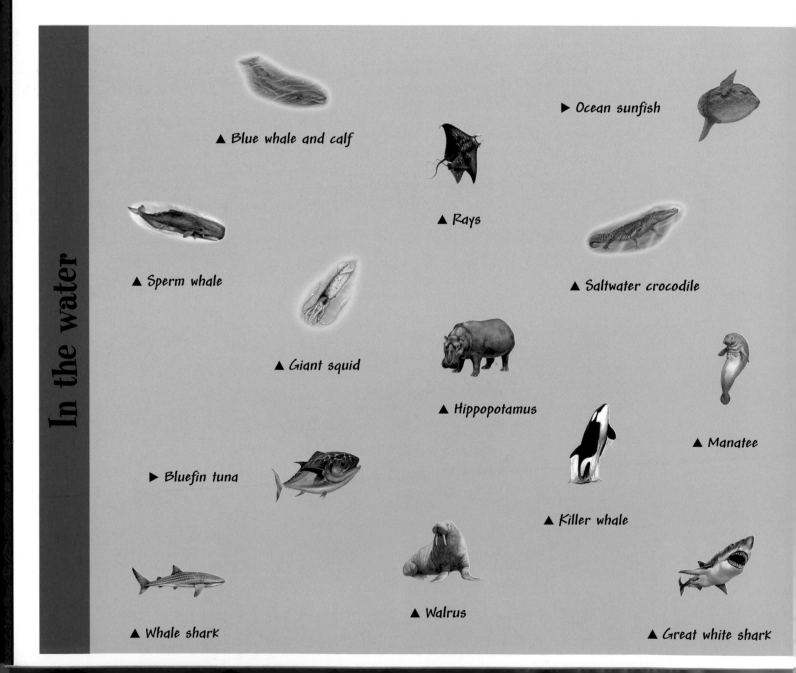

In the water

▲ Blue whale and calf

► Ocean sunfish

▲ Rays

▲ Sperm whale

▲ Saltwater crocodile

▲ Giant squid

▲ Hippopotamus

▲ Manatee

► Bluefin tuna

▲ Killer whale

▲ Walrus

▲ Whale shark

▲ Great white shark

▶ Wandering albatross

▶ Golden eagle

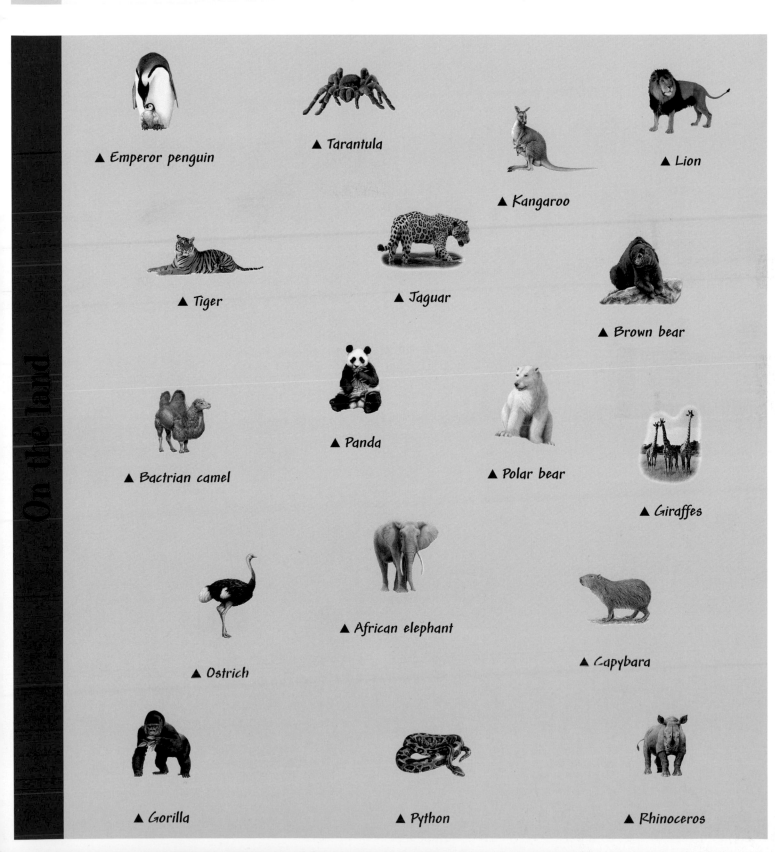

▲ Emperor penguin

▲ Tarantula

▲ Kangaroo

▲ Lion

▲ Tiger

▲ Jaguar

▲ Brown bear

▲ Bactrian camel

▲ Panda

▲ Polar bear

▲ Giraffes

▲ Ostrich

▲ African elephant

▲ Capybara

▲ Gorilla

▲ Python

▲ Rhinoceros

Big animals

▶ Jaguar

These big cats have large, broad heads and muscular bodies

▲ Wandering albatross

This bird has a wingspan of 3.5 metres – it can soar for hours without flapping its wings

◀ Emperor penguin

At 1.2 metres in height, the emperor penguin is also the world's heaviest seabird

◀ Saltwater crocodile

This crocodile is the biggest in the world – it can grow up to 7 metres long!

▶ Kangaroo

Kangaroos may be big but their babies are only 2 centimetres long when born!

▲ Tarantula

Bigger than your hand – this spider is hairy and huge!

▶ Great white shark

This fierce shark swings its tail from side to side to swim at great speeds

▶ Brown bear

When standing on its back legs to see further, the brown bear measures an amazing 3 metres!

KEY:

 In the water

 In the air

 On the land

▲ Whale shark

By far the biggest fish in the ocean, the whale shark can grow up to 12 metres long!

◄ Rhinoceros

Rhinoceroses are extremely strong and well-muscled – they can charge at up to 45 kilometres an hour

◄ Capybara

An excellent swimmer and diver, the capybara is also the world's heaviest rodent

▲ Sperm whale

The world's largest predator at 20 metres long, the sperm whale is over ten times the length of a human!

▼ Tiger

The Siberian tiger is the biggest wild cat – 3.5 metres from nose to tail

◄ Golden eagle

This bird has an enormous wingspan of 6 metres!

► African elephant

The African elephant is the biggest land mammal at about 4 metres tall with a weight of 7.5 tonnes

◄ Giant squid

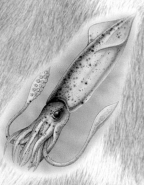

The 15 metre-long giant squid has eyes as big as dinner plates!

The rhea is a large flightless bird of South America – one of its eggs is equivalent to 12 chicken eggs!

Mammal mania!

 The biggest animals in the world on land and sea are both mammals: elephants and whales.

Mammals can adapt brilliantly to different environments. They live almost everywhere, from very high mountain tops to ocean depths, hot deserts and icy cold polar regions.

A mammal's brain is large compared to its body size, suggesting that mammals are one of the most intelligent types of animals. There are many physical differences between mammals – they can have hair, fur, scales or even spikes! However, all mammals have one thing in common – they suckle their young with milk.

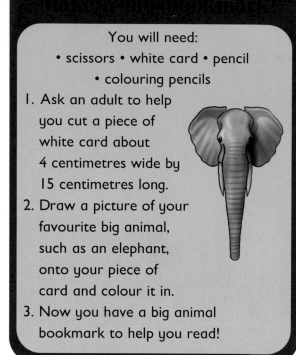

Make a big bookmark!

You will need:
• scissors • white card • pencil
• colouring pencils

1. Ask an adult to help you cut a piece of white card about 4 centimetres wide by 15 centimetres long.
2. Draw a picture of your favourite big animal, such as an elephant, onto your piece of card and colour it in.
3. Now you have a big animal bookmark to help you read!

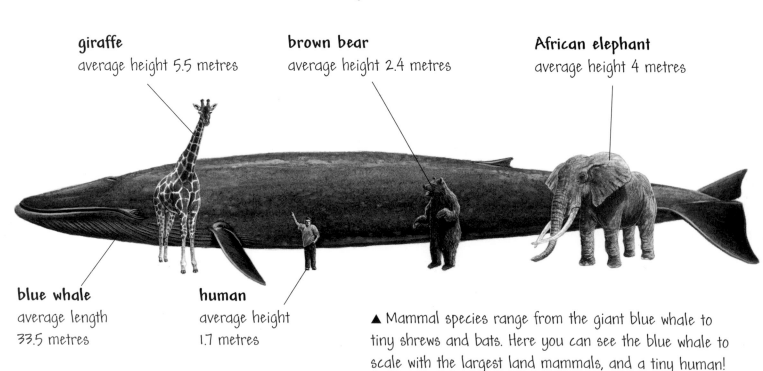

giraffe
average height 5.5 metres

brown bear
average height 2.4 metres

African elephant
average height 4 metres

blue whale
average length 33.5 metres

human
average height 1.7 metres

▲ Mammal species range from the giant blue whale to tiny shrews and bats. Here you can see the blue whale to scale with the largest land mammals, and a tiny human!

▲ Brown bear

▲ Jaguar

▲ Emperor penguin

▲ Tarantula

▲ Wandering albatross

▲ Great white shark

▲ Kangaroo

▲ Saltwater crocodile

Big animals

▼ Tarantula

◄ Great white shark

▼ Brown bear

▶ Saltwater crocodile

▲ Jaguar

▲ Emperor penguin

◄ Kangaroo

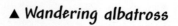

▲ Wandering albatross

▲ Giant squid

▲ Capybara

▲ Whale shark

▲ Tiger

▲ Golden eagle

▲ Rhinoceros

▲ Sperm whale

▲ African elephant

▲ Sperm whale

▲ Giant squid

▼ Golden eagle

▲ Rhinoceros

▲ Whale shark

▲ Capybara

▲ African elephant

▼ Tiger

▲ Polar bear

▲ Lion

▶ Manatee

▶ Killer whale

▲ Bactrian camel

▼ Bluefin tuna

▲ Python

▶ Walrus

▲ Python

▲ Walrus

▲ Lion

▲ Polar bear

▲ Bluefin tuna

▲ Manatee

▲ Killer whale

▲ Bactrian camel

Big animals

▼ Giraffes

▼ Blue whale and calf

▶ Gorilla

▼ Ocean sunfish

▼ Panda

▶ Ostrich

▼ Hippopotamus

▲ Rays

▲ Rays

▲ Panda

▲ Giraffes

▲ Ostrich

▲ Hippopotamus

▲ Gorilla

▲ Ocean sunfish

▲ Blue whale and calf

Grrr!

The brown bear is one of the world's largest predators on land. Males weigh over 600 kilograms and stand almost 3 metres tall. Females are about half the size of males. Brown bears love to eat fish, birds' eggs, honey from bees' nests, wild berries, fruit – in fact just about anything!

By spring, the brown bear has lost half its body weight after hibernation (a long sleep all the way through winter). The bear wakes up and feasts on fish from rivers and streams. Once its decided to catch a fish it doesn't often miss!

Oddly enough not all brown bears are brown. They can be black, light grey, chocolate-coloured or even cream!

▼ The brown bear waits for leaping salmon that swim upstream to breed. It catches them in its powerful jaw or hooks them out with its massive paws.

Big animals

◄ Bactrian camel
This massive animal can go for weeks without water

► Manatee
This water-dwelling mammal measures 4.5 metres long and weighs 1.5 tonnes

► Polar bear
This is the biggest land-based meat eater in the Arctic

◄ Killer whale
This fierce hunter can swim at 55 kilometres an hour – that's pretty fast for an enormous whale!

► Bluefin tuna
A streamlined body means that tuna can swim at speeds of at least 70 kilometres an hour

▲ Lion
The male lion is about 2 metres long not including its tail – which alone measures 1 metre

▼ Walrus
The walrus uses its tusks to drag its heavy body out of the water – tusks can grow up to 1 metre long

◄ Python
The longest snake in the world is a python – it can grow up to 10 metres in length

KEY:

 In the water

In the air

 On the land

◀ Giraffes

A male giraffe is about 5.5 metres tall – that's taller than four people standing on each other's shoulders!

▶ Rays

The manta ray is the world's largest ray with a wing span of 7 metres

▶ Ostrich

Not only is the ostrich the biggest bird at 2.5 metres, it is also lays the biggest eggs!

◀ Panda

They may be big but only 1000 pandas live wild in China – an adult giant panda measures 1.8 metres in length and weighs 100 kilograms

▲ Gorilla

A full-grown male gorilla is about 1.75 metres tall!

◀ Hippopotamus

The hippo is not a good swimmer but it can walk on the riverbed and can stay underwater for up to half an hour

◀ Blue whale and calf

The biggest animal on the planet – the blue whale can measure 30 metres in length

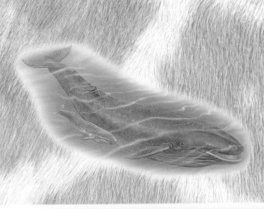

◀ Ocean sunfish

The heaviest bony fish, the sunfish, weighs up to 2 tonnes and measures 4 metres in height!

The African elephant has the biggest nose in the mammal world – it measures up to 2.5 metres long

Biggest and best

Enormous elephants only have four teeth – every year they fall out to be replaced by new ones.

The closest relation to the hippopotamus is the whale!

The camel stores fat in its large humps, which can be used for energy if the camel can't find any food.

Read more facts about big animals around the world

• The blue whale is the largest creature in the world – if you could lift it out of the water and take it home it would make your house seem tiny!

• The female elephant has the longest pregnancy of any mammal – she carries her baby for 21 months. Soon after it is born the calf can stand up, and within a few days it can run.

• The ostrich lays the biggest egg in the world. It weighs 1.5 kilograms, compared to a chicken's egg that weighs 50 grams!

Q: What is the largest ant in the world?
A: An eleph-ant!

Big animals

Discover some amazing facts about big animals

• Pandas have a very specific diet, mainly the shoots and roots of the bamboo plant – they spend half the day eating.

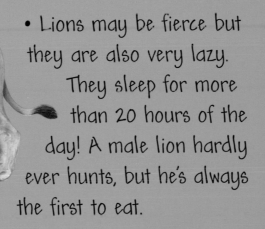

• Lions may be fierce but they are also very lazy. They sleep for more than 20 hours of the day! A male lion hardly ever hunts, but he's always the first to eat.

• The polar bear is specially adapted to survive in cold climates – under its creamy coat is black skin that absorbs heat from the Sun to keep the bear warm.

Q: Why are tigers like army sergeants?
A: They wear stripes!

Fun facts

Manatees are large, slow-moving creatures – they have a very simple diet made up of only plants. To breathe they have to rise to the surface of the water.

At night, gorillas use twigs to build a nest to sleep in.

A giant squid has never been captured alive!

Test your memory!

How much can you remember from your big animal sticker activity book? Find out below!

1. What is the second largest land animal?
2. How many days does a male penguin sit on an egg: 50, 60 or 70?
3. Why does a brown bear stand on its hind legs?
4. When they are born, are kangaroo babies unusually big or small?
5. Which is the biggest big cat: the Bengal tiger, the Sumatran tiger or the Siberian tiger?
6. A brown bear can have a cream-coloured coat: true or false?
7. What do all mammals have in common?
8. What is the largest animal on the planet?
9. Which animal has the longest nose in the world?
10. What are groups of whales called?

Q: What do you call a camel with three humps?
A: Hum-frey!

11. What does a gorilla sleep in at night: a cave, a nest or a hammock?

12. Name two similarities between the rhea and the ostrich.

13. Where does a manatee live: in the air, on the land or underwater?

14. How many teeth does an elephant have?

15. What colour is a polar bear's skin?

16. Which sea creature has never been captured alive?

17. How many hours a day do lions spend sleeping?

18. What is the name of the tiny sea creatures that blue whales eat?

19. What does a walrus use its giant tusks to help it do?

20. What special feature helps the bluefin tuna swim fast: a streamlined body, a big mouth or good eyesight?

🐼 The long trunk of an elephant is made up of 40,000 different muscles!

🐼 The blue whale has the biggest baby – when it is born the calf is already 7 metres long!

🐼 The ostrich can run really fast, up to 70 kilometres an hour, but it can't fly at all!

Answers:

1. Rhino 2. 60 3. To see further 4. Small
5. Siberian tiger 6. True 7. All mammal babies suckle milk
8. Blue whale 9. Elephant 10. A pod
11. A nest 12. Both birds can't fly and lay giant eggs
13. Underwater 14. 4 15. Black 16. Giant squid 17. 20
18. Krill 19. Climb out of the water 20. A streamlined body

Q: How do elephants talk to each other?
A: On the 'elephone!

www.animalplanet.co.uk

10 STICKER FUN BOOKS TO COLLECT

Animal Planet is all things animal.

Like an animal itself, Animal Planet is gripping, instinctual, exciting and alive. Animal Planet tells real-life stories with animals in the lead roles. You can see the personality of each animal shine through, reminding us how much we have in common with those that share our planet.